CRICK! CRACK!

THE BONFIRE COLLECTIVE

CONTENTS

THE STORY CIRCLES FROM TELLER TO LISTENER

by Opal Palmer Adisa

A story comes into being only if there is a teller, Crick.

In order for a story to have life and have meaning there must be a listener, Crack.

Teller and listener are essential for storytelling to take place and the active participation of both is necessary for the story's enfoldment.

Stories are really about a community sharing its values, its loves and its hopes. The stories (poems and prose) in this collection are about a community of writers who are family and friends, and colleagues and supporters whose stories speak to each other, and sometimes speak against one another.

When connection is a natural stream, rather than forged, it works more fluidly, unfolding on its own. How it happens I am not sure, but we tend to know when we connect with someone, with that person's story, which in fact means we have connected with that person's life. These are writers that I connect with viscerally, spiritually, lines collapsing between teacher and students, running into friendship based on mutual respect, admiration and dare I say love. Language was what connected us initially, getting entangled in the fissure of words, the semantics of syntax, the labyrinth of meanings, the dance of recognition, the blessings of voice—their stories, what was going on in their lives, their loves and fears, their abandonment, joy, and optimistic hold on a future. They were working at being writers. Charming! Nobel! Foolish even, but so right for who they are and are being. Crick! Crack!

The stories circle back to history and culture, which for us is a Sunday afternoon in my backyard enjoying the sun, writing, breaking bread together as food is intrinsic, and catches them/us in a loop of memory, imagining imaginings, unfurling experiences and the swell of words through which we swim in search of meaning, or perhaps just the dream—forever illusive and ethereal.

Not unlike Adam's little girl, lost in her own musing, seeking adventure only to have it snatched from her by a father, long given up on himself. Does she succumb to an early death or find a hole and peer through. Crick! Find her by your feet and ask her to share what is still unbroken in her.

Andrew's story takes on a more matter-of-fact air, allowing us to see him—the pro-tagonist as a somewhat eccentric, obsessive knife lover, prone to accidents, or per-haps his complete participation in life does not always allow for safe passage. Crack! How does he negotiate his way when life's spices stream into his blood.

In truth it is said there is only one story, the same story that has been reworked and altered, stretched and shrunken, beaten up and mended, reworked to resemble all our lives. We know this is so in Anne's story as Virginia meets herself at an age she thought was so far ahead of her. She is neither amused nor daunted. Both possibili-ties exist for her and both are true.

And the story continues to loop in Jack's piece, bring us smack close and personal to the smell of our own breath. We come face-to-face with that painful moment when no language has currency, when no word sheds meaning, when getting in touch with pain is as necessary as breath, and breathing and tears are what take you through the journey back to your own self. Crick! Crack? The stories about your various antics that your parents love to tell, while you slide down in the chair, getting smaller and smaller until there is no place to go, to disappear until you decide. You are either present or have absconded.

Then there is loss, and there is loss whose tail is always behind and the spinning around is dizzying, which is the feeling Lyndsey gives us as we peer in on Daphne, whose story of mother/daughter relationship, fraught as they often are, is so old, yet so new and distinct. It's a story with the backside exposed, as if the story is wearing a hospital gown, walking downtown, unaware everyone is pointing and gawking at it.

Until nature, not plant-life, but the natural inevitableness of life runs its script as it does in Livia's piece in which the haunting transition from high school to what's next forces these teenagers' hand, or perhaps nature is innocent and lustful desire is just a renegade defying time's consistent rhythm.

Although it might seem as if it came out of no where, Myron's escape in the canal is yet another story of near-misses, elevated to adventure and an opportunity in the future to brag, but also consider the what if possibility—stories that travel down the path of narcissism and God-playing scope—yet the real story stands side-by-side with alternate endings, cricking and cracking all over the place.

In the hands of an artist a story is a lesson, a lesson becomes a lecture, a lecture turns into a face slap, exposing you to what you don't know, but also as Nana so craftily points out, locating the pain and shame you should feel, but feeling has been so long absent from your sphere, you see it and think it a smug at best, or something useless to be tossed.

Circle back. No go forward, just a little. No take a step back. Right there in Shela-na's story the past greets the present and they discover they are strangers who have traveled the same path, carrying the same bag in which are the same Ola leaves, your story, her story, his story, their stories, all the stories are there, safe as always, waiting for you to carry them forward, keeping grandmother's voice a whistle that bounces from one tree to the next deep in the forest.

The story is decent when the teller is as eager to tell it as the listeners are enthusias-tic to hear it and together they create a tight space where the story can be born and can grow, even with a sixth finger and not feel odd in a five-finger hand world.

When you open this collection you will find stories that are waiting for you, that greet you with familiarity and newness and take you where you might have gone, but show you things you had not seen. Crick. We gather in a classroom. Initially strangers. But that state quickly gives way to communion. Crick we settle at the beach and read the stars. Crick we peel back the skin and bite. Crack. You bring some of yourself to the table. You eat even though your hands are dirty. Crack. The story spins around searching for its tail and tale. Someone steps on it. Another slices it off, but the story keeps going, yarn unreeling, linking them to me, me to them, us to you, you to them. Crick...Read. Read on. Read some more. No become the story! Crack! You say Crack! Pass it on. Tell the story that is you.

THE PALM

By Shelana deSilva

My grandmother left this behind. It's a story in pictures, scratched onto ola leaves. I don't know which tale it depicts, but there is the Buddha. I recognize his placid face and solar halo. I remember seeing stacks of ola leaf books in the temple. They were long and thin and looked like wooden blinds drawn tight and laid length-wise on dusty shelves. The stacks tilted this way and that. The dust between them was the oldest dust on earth. There were hundreds of them sleeping in the gloom—a strange library. After my grandmother died, I found this story on ola leaves sleeping in her bureau. It's a smaller version of the texts in the temple, no longer than your palm. Little slats of dried ola leaf, scratched pictures depicting some Buddhist story, Grantha text on the back, each panel sits on top of the other. When you open the book, lifting the rough-hewn wooden cover, the overlapping slats stand up, strung together with ancient thread.

Ola leaf books are made from the green, fibrous leaves of the Talipot palm, *Corypha umbraculifera*, which bears the biggest inflorescence of any plant—the most massive cluster of flowers on the same stem. These blooms grow up to twenty-six feet long and consist of millions of tiny white flowers that wave from a few branched stalks reaching from the top of the palm's trunk, up through the leaves, sitting like a gi-ant plumed hat on the tree's head. The Talipot palm starts this magnificent display when it is between thirty and eighty years old. No one understands the timing of this singular phenomenon. After flowering it fruits, producing thousands of round yellow-green drupes the size of apricots, each containing a single hard seed. After it has completed this sequence, the Talipot palm will die.

I am sure my grandmother knew the legend depicted in this ola leaf book, found hidden among her things. No matter how many times I look through it, I cannot decipher the tale. I know it must be a good story—here is the Buddha with a forlorn woman combing her long hair, an elephant with graceful tusks is saddled off to the side; here is the Buddha in lotus pose with a demon approaching, clawed, fanged and armored; here is a two-headed, fire-breathing dragon coiled at the Buddha's feet; here the Buddha sits in a resplendent hall, his palm held high to bless two people and strangely, a huge rat. The three figures kneel in worship.

Who knows how a tale begins, who first told it, wrote it down? When I hold some-thing very old in my hand, I wonder who has held it before me, who might hold it again. Like this ola leaf book, a story has an unpredictable life. It could be recog-nizable to some, indecipherable to others. It is fragile, old and has seen more of the world than you or me.

IT WAS ESSENTIAL

By Shelana deSilva

Things green, like fiddleheads prehistoric and verdant,
begin to grow in the tightly packed black soil.
Closed hard, turned in on themselves,
yet pushing skyward.
The terrestrial hue of new life shows through the dirt
like so many small elbows.
Meteorite sprigs become tender shoots, eventually.
Somehow these plants, these green things, are just beginning.

ALONG THE WAY

By Shelana deSilva

CRICK! CRACK!

Wind-battered pine cones,
wet and wine-dark,
thrown from boughs.
Some are chipped like teeth.
There is the smell of water and
suddenly, a winter sky

CHURCH

By Shelana deSilva

weighted with water,
leaves slip from their lines.
they drop to the forest floor,
a tangle of castoffs.
layer after layer forms there
hiding an historical account
of wet years, drought years, unseasonal winds,
the bones of visiting creatures,
mammalian droppings, insect shells,
blind seeking worms,
dirt and fibric peat—
the growing goes both up and down,
sometimes latticed with roots
or anchored by patient stones.

what liturgy takes place here?
what can i take back
to the other trespassers?

the canopy above,
diffusing carbonated light,
the spongy ground absorbing transmissions—
another leaf falls.
an unmarked moment,
one of many.
this place keeps
growing/decaying,
being what it is.

there is a pattern,
a cycle,

there exists a balance between rot and renewal.
the forest explains it all—
repeating the principles again and again,
throughout time,
for those who would listen.

KNIVES OF THE OLD WORLD

By Andrew Gori

I cut myself on my new knives, my birthday knives, but no blood came out. The knives were a gift from my wife, Nadia, and I had just taken them out of the box. There were six in total, each with its own utility, and they were sheathed in plastic and cardboard. I had already pulled five from their wrapping and dumped them into the sink when the paring knife slid from my grip and sliced my index finger. But there was no blood.

I would not tell Nadia. She told me it was dangerous to ask for knives as a gift because fate could turn them against me. Nadia was born in Russia, raised with a sensitivity for the ancient world and better understands our connection to it. She told me I would have to think of something else that I needed, but I couldn't, so an agreement was made; I would pick out the knives and "buy" them from her for a penny. And just in case fate was hip to our plan, she would buy me some comic books to emphasize that the knives were not my gift. Later that night Nadia called long distance to Russia and held a thunderous palaver with her mother. I watched from the couch and after she hung up the phone, she knelt at my side and rested her elbows on my lap.

"It's still bad luck, even if you buy them," she said, shaking her head.

I went into the kitchen and grabbed a tomato and the sharpest knife I had.

"Look," I said, then started to slice. The knife barely pierced the tomato's skin and I had to push down on it so much, it burst open and spit out a pink, watery cluster of seeds.

My display was as effective as any infomercial and she reluctantly gave in. Nadia bought the knives the next day and before leaving the store, I handed her a penny. She gave me the knives and we shook hands. When we got home, she left to buy my comic books while I stayed to clean the knives. But I couldn't, because I sliced open a wound that would not bleed. I held the corrupted finger over the sink and simmered in the layers of irony. I would tell Nadia; this was too funny not to.

That's when the finger began to ooze blood: thick, dark blood that made me think the cut had been deep. I rushed into the bathroom and cleaned my finger with soap and hot water, spread some disinfectant on the wound and dressed it with a small band-aid. Remembering my Boy Scout training, I held my hand over my head, decreasing the blood flow and giving my finger a chance to heal. Satisfied, I returned to the kitchen and cleaned my new knives. Some of them were coated with blood, so they had to be cleaned better than the others.

I finished cleaning the knives and decided to take a quick nap on my couch. Just as I was falling asleep, I heard a small bang from behind my stove. I lurched up but stayed where I was. My apartment makes noises. There is the wet hissing sound, like a teakettle, that flares up under the sink. Sometimes the fridge clanks like metal pipes banging together. Most frequently is the bang behind the stove, like something small and fierce is trapped in the walls and every now and again gathers enough strength to try and break free. The first night I spent there I was convinced someone was trying to break in, so I turned on all the lights and put "Chinatown" in my DVD player and blasted the volume. I've come to accept that the noises were here before me and there is nothing to be done about them. I lay back on the couch and stared at the ceiling.

When I hear the noises, I think I understand the ancient world, the world that demands I buy the knives or else a little better. I wonder what our ancestors, for whom every step was venturing into a new frontier did when noises woke them up at night. Maybe they made up rules to keep themselves calm. The rules worked and they became law until enough time passes that nobody remembered why. But I take no comfort in these thoughts because the noises are still real and just as scary.

When Nadia came home, she nodded her head towards my band-aid and looked at me with wide eyes.

"Oh, that? Those knives are very sharp," I said. "Don't say anything."

"I don't need to," she said, laughing and shaking her head.

A few hours later some friends stopped by so we could have a drink before we met some more people for dinner at a nice Ethiopian restaurant on the other side of Golden Gate Park. We drank wine and I showed everyone my comic books and knives and those who knew me best were able to make the connection between a new set of knives and a fresh bandage on my finger. When it was time to go, I rushed into the bathroom and slowly peeled away the band-aid. The wound underneath was thick and syrupy with sweat and clotted blood. I washed it again and put on fresh dressing.

The air in the park was thick and cool, and felt like an empty glove caressing my chin. My finger throbbed with its own pulse, but I was just drunk enough not to care. We walked past an empty fountain with a statue of a lion battling a giant lizard. I asked where the scene came from but nobody knew. Probably some Greek myth, I thought.

We got to the restaurant. It was warm inside and there was a giant table set up for us in the back. Dinner was communal and placed on one large plate in the middle of the table. Instead of silverware everyone was given a piece of spongy flatbread that is used to pick up the meat and vegetables from the communal plate. Most of the food was rich with spicy, oily sauces that dribbled down my fingers and seeped through the band-aid. It stung, but I had resolved myself to ignore the pain and enjoy my dinner. Surely if there are unseen forces in the world, some must be benevolent.

After dinner we walked back through the park. It was late and we were the only
people in view. It had gotten considerably colder over the few hours we had spent
in the restaurant and when my friends spoke, their breath looked like translucent
sheets of cotton. Nadia shivered, and when I asked her if she needed my sweater, she
said she wasn't cold.

We got home and when I turned on the light, nothing happened.

"You just changed that bulb," Nadia said, shaking her head.

"It's the curse of the knives," I said, then made an "oooooh" sound.

"You are a very funny person," she said without smiling. "I'm getting in the shower."

The sound of running water filled the living room as I changed the light bulb. I had
forgotten to turn the light switch off, and when I twisted the bulb in, the light came
on with a blinding glare. I almost fell off the chair I had been standing on and when
the spots cleared from my eyes, I saw that I was hovering over the dish rack where I
had left my knives to dry. I would not tell Nadia.

EVERYONE AT HOME

By Adam Moskowitz

Mom comes home to cook. The kitchen steams. She wears a dirty apron and a red bandana. She drinks red wine and eats a big bar of dark chocolate. She chops things, and things sizzle, and you can smell it.

Morty is our cat. She calls him Mortimer when he hops onto the counter. When she turns on the immersion blender, Morty hides under the big, plaid sofa.

Dad's hands are always green and dirty. That's because he cuts grass. All his clothes have layers of grass stains on them. His fingers are really big, like they are all different kinds of thumbs. He has a big, red truck. Del used to help Dad. He rode in the passenger seat of the truck. He used the backpack blowers and the small mower, while Dad rode on the big mower. Now, Burt rides in the passenger seat. Burt is just as old as Dad. Dad and Burt call the truck the Big Red Bitch.

Del and I made a deal. The deal is that Del pays me a dollar each time I talk to a girl. If I don't talk to any, I get a Dead Arm. "Don't make me get all Krav Maga on you," says Del. Del knows a lot of Self-Defense Systems, and his Dead Arms are no joke. They hurt like hell. But Del says he's only given me the sissy ones. He threatens that if I ever make him really mad, he'll have to break out the Close Combat Dead Arm. I looked up the Close Combat Dead Arm online, but nothing came up.

WHEN I INVENTED THE TIME GAME

By Adam Moskowitz

My Timex wraps my wrist like a big belt. I press its buttons. I change it to Military Time so that I can think I'm in the military. I whisper, "We'll head to the bridge soon." I leave it in Military Time for a minute, but switch it right back. This is always what happens when I put it into Military Time. Del knows how to tell Military Time.

Here's how I play the Time Game. I look at the second digits and see how long I can look at a second before it ends. If I see it end, I lose the round. If I can look at a second and look away before it changes, I win the round. I try to catch the longest part of each second. I try to look at the second right after it starts so I can have the most time with it. Sometimes, I win. I catch it right after it changes because it feels like time stops, and I'm breathing with my pulse. Like I'm alone and alive. I play the Time Game on my Timex.

I remember when I invented the Time Game. Del and I were waiting on a train platform, and there was this little girl. She hugged her dad's knee, and swung around leaning back all the way. Her mom watched her swing. She smiled, stopped. Her dad had a tattoo of a vine and it was crawling up his whole arm. There was a sword in the thick part of his arm. The sword was tied up in the vine, and the vine was bleeding.

We were the only ones down there, and Del was all quiet, and I was watching the little girl swing. The train came, and the sound was scary, and Del said, "Remember when you used to think that sound was scary?" We got to pick our seats, and Del started to doze off. The girl started to climb the pole that people hold inside the train. The mom watched, but the dad got up and pulled her down and sat her down, and the girl was quiet. Del was already asleep.

I looked down at my Timex. It looked like the second was frozen before it changed. It was at fifty-six. I invented the Time Game right then and there. I started playing. I lost three rounds. Then I won. I looked away right before twelve ended. It was the longest second of all time. I breathed out on the glass of the watch, and wiped it with the soft part of my sweatshirt, the inside part.

I used to have a Casio. The Casio had a light that you could turn on by pressing a little metal button. The light was for telling the time at night. I used it for other things too. I pretended I was trapped in a cave. I pretended I was prepared with my watch light to help me escape. I pretended to stumble over cave things, like sharp, wet rocks shaped like cones. I pretended that the light on the watch helped me dodge hanging bats.

I don't use the light on my Timex. I want to save the power of the bulb. I like turning off lights. I like knowing lights are off and I like watching them dim first, like they're falling asleep. I think they're always getting too hot and are always waiting to be turned off.

At night, I run around the living room and kitchen. I slide across the floors on my thick tube socks, finding lights. I find bright, empty bathrooms. I find dripping sinks. I make sure the refrigerator is closed. "At least someone in this house cares about the electric bill," says Dad. I don't. I care about electricity pumping hard between the layers of the walls, blue and squiggly, like what the emperor shoots out of his hands in Return of the Jedi. I worry that too much of it races through the walls. I like turning things off. I imagine our whole house sighing.

THE BIG RED TRUCK

By Adam Moskowitz

Mom is cooking green beans, and I wish she wasn't. I secretly wrap green beans up in napkins, go to the bathroom and flush them down the toilet during dinner. I don't like to do this because I want to like vegetables, and I want to like them because they are good for me. I want to invent a strand of vegetables that tastes like cookies.

I look for Del to tell him about the girls at school. There was Nancy from Geography. We were sitting in class, and something dropped near my right foot, next to Nancy's left foot. It was in the corner of my eye. I thought that if I looked she would think I was weird because I'd be looking at her foot. I looked anyway. "Can I help you?" she whispered like she was screaming at the same time. I looked at the thing, which was a hair band. I didn't want to sound to her like she did to me, so I tried to whisper differently. "Can I have that hair thing?" I said. I said this just so I could say something. She looked like she thought I was weird.

Then there was Lauren. I liked her because the shape of her hair is the same as the shape of her face. I asked Lauren if people call her Laura for short. Then I realized Lauren doesn't have more syllables than Laura. Plus, it's a totally different name. I don't know what kind of Dead Arm it was, but Del got me bad.

I decided that since I was trying to talk to girls, I must be getting older, and so I ate all the green beans. I decided that if I was getting older, I should probably stop playing the Time Game. I played one last round, and it was easy to win.

I got in bed and looked at the ceiling. I used to imagine that God lived in a wooden house that looked like our well outside. I could never see God, only his little wooden house. I imagined seeing my hidden version of God on my ceiling. When I tried to sleep, I pretended that my bed could slide out of the house. It grew these heavy-duty tires, and I could drive it out of the woods. Then I could even float it above the streets of the town, and I could see the streets. They looked like curvy rivers. I would make my way to the ocean. My bed would grow glass walls. I'd plop my bed into the ocean and I would wander around underwater. I wouldn't really see anything or look for anything. It would be dark in the ocean and nothing would know I was there. It was just the place where I would sleep. Before falling asleep, I would hear the sound of being surrounded by water, which is a very quiet sound.

In the morning, I hear Burt outside. I hear the truck in the driveway. Dad warms it up. I like to know that he doesn't just drive it without doing that. It's loud when he leaves, and I hear Del in his room rolling around.

WRECKING BALL PENDULUM

By Myron Michael

We were in the canals—
before the bulldozers came
and the wrecking crew came—
swimming through shallow water and
                    seeing through green glow,
holding our breath.   Using our arms like fins,
in one way   out another,
we swam like pike   through and through.

The wrecking ball swung,
its pendulum struck the amphitheatre
like a clock's hand strikes a number.
Yellow bricks were dislodged,
a timeline of patrons broken.
The practice of children playing Jacque Cousteau
canceled. Green water drained
into sewers, maybe, into Grand River—
                    No swimming there;
bloated flesh tumbled over the fish ladder.

It wasn't all a loss:
the old amphitheatre received a facelift,
and the memories of swimming
beneath its bridges as a child
are worth keeping:
my cousin's knees scraped the yellow brick
bottom of the plaza's pool—
where by-passers pitched pennies
that carried the wishes of husbands and wives
for marriages to last; for fortune to trip them up
like an untied shoelace, the wish for just
a little less inhibition, faces to the floor—
my cousin didn't cry, he was as tough a swimmer
as he was a linebacker; he licked the scratches
on his knee with a wet finger and smiled at me.

CHANGE BY FIRE

By Myron Michael

The landscape changes, and we change.
As the tree doesn't remember the storefront,
neither do we remember how the fire started.

There was a bottle,
fragmentation of a window
several blocks away,
speculation: fire trucks and police cars.
A morning after.

A mound of dirt, a tractor
men worked, a woman on the inside looked on
from her suitcase, called an accountant,
assessed the damage, stepped over footprints
it'd taken twenty years to make.

It could've been a cigarette butt or
an electrical problem.

As the grass doesn't remember the water
nor the rubber boots,
neither do we remember
the incense that fell off the counter
and onto the rug, nor
that the tired old man forgot
to turn off the pilot-light
beneath a pan of grease in the flat above.

AUTOBIOGRAPHY IN PARTS

By Myron Michael

excerpts from Childhood

I.

The police came when my mother pointed. My father
vanished like smoke in a mirror. *When's he coming back?*
I asked. *Never*, she shrugged. ~~The heat of the moment~~
~~taught me how~~ One miracle doesn't compare to another,
and a magic trick done with slight of hand can't undo itself.
Fire like time moves quickly, that I learned
while conjuring smoke from a family portrait ~~my father~~
~~tried to cut short her life by driving a knife three inches~~
~~from her heart through her back.~~ *Metal doesn't break, it*
bends. How's that for transformation? she smiled, turning
the Biblical page where those hurt on earth are healed in heaven.

2.

It was like holding the pith of fire in my hands.
To make a tub of water boil, I put them on its faucet
then turned—~~Classmates called me Freddy~~ I fought...
~~to mean my hands gave them nightmares~~ and was served
cool kisses from girls twirling rope who learned in class
that I was no push over but, acrobatic with acrostics—
~~pushing out each metric poem with Shakespearean surge~~
my tongue was as hot as my head which meant my words
were on fire as well and possibly, the reason my knees
struck like matchsticks and made extra pockets in my jeans
my mother, in line at the Salvation Army, called fashion.

3.

The gurney was smooth as paper and cold. The oxygen mask
smelled of alcohol. The medic said, "What flavor?"
I thought of a red Blow Pop my sister gave me one afternoon
I beat her at a game of badminton in the backyard
of a duplex with red bricks in Benton Harbor. I thought of her
to get back to ~~where she was at~~ that apartment
~~where the lazy man in a mask was practicing~~
~~Halloween tricks~~. I said, *Cherry* and there she was
at the side of my gurney in the arms of my mother, crying.

4.

Welcome home! Everyone shouted. I was in a tan suit
that made me itch. There was an Atari 2600 on a table,
just for me. A chocolate cake, just for me. Balloons
and a piñata, just for me and the cousins I'd share Blow
Pops with. It wasn't my birthday, but the day I came to.
God has shown his mercy. Thank you, Jesus! my aunt
praised. We sang *Amazing Grace*; I cut the cake.

OF A HOUSE THAT ISN'T MINE

By Myron Michael

Let its doors swing open.
Its floors
go where they lead a life.
No road signs where walls are
worn through like carpet.
They indeed speak,
hold echoes, no apologies.
What is taken is took
and brought up.
Shoulder silence
that follows tears, contempt
for yellow wallpaper.
Punches from a life
that once stood here or there crying,
growing beyond measurements on plaster,
soft laughter broken when bodies touch.

SEVEN'S ENOUGH

By Jack Bergquist

My son is nothing but a memory now. His letter arrived early one afternoon, in a business sized envelope. I threw out the rest of the mail, all junk, and brought his letter to the bathroom. I read and reread it, many times I think, long after having moved my bowels. After some time, I removed all my clothing for no particular reason, and sat there, drifting between dreams and reality.

When my son was little he used to wake me up on mornings when heavy snow had fallen the night before. Until age ten or so, I would let him jump out of his bedroom window, on the second floor, whenever a foot or more of snow was on the ground. Sometimes he would build little snow banks and do flips into them. The neighbors thought his mother and I were crazy, but what did they know? He knew how to land properly. His bedroom is now a guestroom, down the hall from where I opened his letter.

Sitting on the toilet, completely naked, I could hear my wife standing opposite the door. Her fingernails rapped softly against the door's hollow pine. "Honey," she moaned. Such rudeness. Not to interrupt a man in the bathroom is surely a timeless rule. And so few are the rules that remain timeless. It broke my dream of snowfalls and jumping from windows, and brought me back to my senses. I ignored her calls and closed my eyes, trying to picture my son again. I imagined his death, the suicide that he described in his note. I imagined him in his final moment, calm... ready to leave this world, and the deathly silence that must have filled his head just before he pressed the gun to his temple. Time slowed down for me the way it often does during near death experiences. I felt calm and relaxed, and justified in telling my wife to piss off, but that's irony, yeah? I felt I deserved to be alone in that moment, but she wanted to talk. We hadn't been talking much of late, which was sort of nice. And just as I was getting used to the recent disconnect in our relationship, she now wanted to get along famously.

I'm not exactly sure what happened next, in part because the moment itself is not much more than a haze to begin with. But certain spots are clear as day. I know I didn't breathe. I clenched up. My wife was now standing silently outside the bathroom door. I remember trying to hear what she was doing, as if listening hard enough would create a sound. I heard her breathing slow down. My body tensed more, and it hurt. I could have been sitting there for hours, like those moments when you awake in the morning and your mind jumps from what to wear to work, back to dreams just below consciousness. But the way time passed in the bathroom—in my dreamlike state—was enough to tell me that I had been at least semi-conscious since opening the suicide note. Or maybe I was just having dreams based in reality, dreams I couldn't control. I don't know. Sometimes when you toss and turn all night, you get up in the morning and aren't sure whether or not you ever fell asleep. Time passes extremely slowly at first, but then all of a sudden it's morning. Maybe you were awake the whole time, or maybe you were dreaming that you were awake. Reading a suicide note on the toilet bore a strange resemblance to this dreamlike semi-consciousness.

My wife continued rapping quietly on the door, though I didn't answer. Sound became a constant white-noise, the sleepless night that fades into day while you do nothing but wait for something to happen, hoping for either sleep or the morning, though you know neither will come for a long while. My vision became a picture that I viewed without recognition. I knew it to be there, but it had no message, no meaning. I was living something more surreal than any dream. Meanwhile, my wife had found her way into my periphery. When she entered, I was staring at the door with my head propped on one hand, the note in the other. I let go of my son's suicide note for the first time since opening it. It fell by my feet. She picked it up and began to read. My elbows pressed into my thighs, my head slowly sliding through my hands, toward the ground. My wife stood directly over me, her knees touching mine. Tears formed in her eyes and dropped to her pink carpet. My head hung so near the carpet now that I could nearly see the fibers of her pink, dirty, wormy toilet-mat, turning red with her tears. My son was twenty-seven years old.

The moment hung and my eyes buzzed as if the flash of a camera had just gone off. I wondered if my son had followed through with his threat. Maybe someone had stopped him. My mind became still.

Suddenly my wife grabbed me. It felt like a beautiful dream interrupted, yes it did. I tried my best to remain detached, but my wife's cheeks rubbed against mine. Her tears smeared my face. I mumbled to myself: "fuck fuck fuck," which helped me to forget my son for a moment, but it did not help get rid of this very alive, crying, moaning, mother of his. The fuck of it was her whining. I pushed her away, and the room became still for another instant. The imprints on my thighs deepened where my elbows pressed down. She tried to pull my hands from my face, and I told her to fuck off.

I wanted to cut my nerve endings. Looking back, I think I feared being able to process the whole thing, although that is precisely all I really hoped to do, to be able to process the thing. What bothered me most that day was that my reaction was much like others I've had with death, because death comes often. It's an inevitable occurrence that finds me largely unemotional. His note said not to call and not to worry, since there was nothing his mother or I could do. Johnson, our son, was so calm in dire circumstance.

There are probably some things about his note I should relate before I bury him in my mind. It addressed his mother twice: once referring to his regret for his actions, and again to say that he loves her and to express his sorrow. He knew to spare me such trifling. He addressed me mostly to explain things; not because he was cold or insensitive, but for brevity, and to spare me sentimentality. But he does explain things. I still become somehow enamored with him whenever I read his letter, always searching for something hidden in his message. Maybe I am fishing for something that I'll never find, but one thing I know for certain is that he was serious about his decision. It was not some whim.

He purchased the gun at a local game and tackle store: it took only a few days to acquire. He was a relatively clean boy with a clean record. He purchased a carton of bullets, and threw all but one away, said his note. The police report stated that he sat down outside his local ER, put the gun to his temple and pulled the trigger without hesitating.

He planned his course of action well, almost too well, which consoles me. At least he had his wits about him. In the time it took for his letter to travel three thousand miles from his corner mail box in Spokane, WA, to our house in Bald Head, ME— yes, Bald Head, that's the name of the town in which we raised him: population 1,565—he had also been writing letters to his friends, explaining the reasons for his decision. He wrote to some friends before us, then to us, then other friends. In his state he could not prioritize people, he said, even his mother and me. The psychology of having your mother and father and far away friends be with you throughout your days, like your breath, was forever foreign and absurd to him. Mind-blowing, he joked. He was alone, as he preferred to be.

He wrote in his note, *Doctors do not yet perform brain transplants, or else I would certainly send the bullet through my heart. But since doctors transplant the heart—along with seven other organs—it becomes more valuable than the brain when my body is clinically dead. I always preferred logic to emotion, so I terminate the brain, not the heart, however odd that may sound. In any case, that makes eight potentially useful organs I leave. It's funny how facts change somewhere between life and death. My mind tells me that my mind is of no use when I'm dead so that's where I put the bullet, such a thoughtful bullet.*

My periphery caught his mother reading this section of the letter. She did not think it funny that Johnson used a thoughtful bullet.

She slimed my face again. Her tears slid around my cheeks, forming a mucus. And I was left comparing his mother's slime to my son's brains oozing down the back of his body, lifeless and limp, sort of like what my body must have looked like on the shitter. I believe Johnson is having some fun with me now. Could he have pictured this scene? He knows I read the mail while shitting. A last joke between men. A smile grew on my face, which suddenly began to hurt. His mother had punched me with her rings on. Blood dripped from my mouth and nose, turning another spot on her carpet red, then another, then another. Then she embraced me, smearing blood across my face.

"What is wrong with you?" she said.

"Me?"

She saw the blood smeared on my cheek... The moment hung like the others. My genitals were still exposed. Fluids were everywhere. The light was constant and relentless...

She slowly backed out of the bathroom.

I picked up the letter where she had dropped it, and read it again. He was our only child.

During adolescence, a heart murmur had developed in him, which prevented him from participating on his high school baseball team in any role, even bat boy. He attended every game, though, and played in pick up games with people who didn't know he had a heart defect. Just days before killing himself, Johnson had researched the details of organ donation. Despite his defect, there was still a small chance that his heart could be transferable. So, just in case, the bullet opened up his face, and not his heart, which would have been a tad less messy.

Johnson's letter continued,

Including the heart, I could save up to eight lives, but seven's enough. Who wants eight of me running around, anyway? I don't want even one. Finally, on my last legs, irony is clear.

A droplet of my blood hit the page, directly on the word *last*, making the page read *on my legs, irony is clear.* Yes Johnson, I thought, irony is clear. No tears from me, just blood.

After washing up and getting dressed, I pocketed the letter and yelled through the house that I was going for a walk. My wife was probably curled in some corner. I didn't think of her because I was thinking about the letter. The difficulty with which suicide letters are supposedly written is not evident in Johnson's. It is presumed to be the author's penultimate act in life, which in essence is cliché, and this is devastating. No one wants their second to last act on earth to be cliché.

I left his mother behind and exited our house. His note calmed me as I walked down the street. I read his final words without looking where I was going. It read:

This is a decision I feel I have the right to make without explaining to no end, since it is, by nature, infinitely complicated. But in short: My misery ends. Yours and mom's begins. Seven or eight people's lives are dramatically saved. Two—yours and mom's—hurt. Numbers seem to side with me. Morality may side against me, depending on who you believe. What would John Stuart Mill think? It doesn't matter now anyhow. I would write more but I must attend to other letters. Take care and carry on, I am so sorry.

Love,

Your son.

From behind I heard my wife running toward me, and I too felt the strong urge to run.

SECOND TIME

By Livia Ching

Outside the sun is shining. Inside the air is cool and chills her feet. She walks through the house in a thin striped skirt and a shabby boys tunic, believing this mismatched outfit will keep her warm. Deep in a reverie, she does not feel hunger or thirst (two forces she rarely neglects). As the sun drifts down from the highest point in the sky, she waits for the appointment. The neighborhood is nearly abandoned at this time of day, save the gardeners blowing leaves and the elderly who take their morning and afternoon walks like clockwork.

A spot polished Karmann Ghia with creeps of copper showing between the curves puts its way into her parents' driveway. She tucks a tendril of hair behind her ear, paces between the couch and a cold fireplace. The door of the glorified jalopy he drives to capture females like unsuspecting bumblebees opens and shuts. As she listens quietly to the sounds of his impending approach, the tips of her fingers and toes tingle and lose warmth. Blood is traveling back to those areas he's touched before. His strides are long and quick. He tries to hide his tremors by knocking hard on the weatherworn front door. Upon hearing of his arrival, she reluctantly places her frozen feet into soft silk slippers meant for house guests, not for hosts. Meanwhile, she's noticed that her nipples have hardened and that the skin of her thighs have become warmer than her limbs.

They are old friends but the embrace is somehow new. Only two weeks after graduating from high school, he is already bored with life. While she is in a great hurry to cross over experience thresholds before she leaves for college so no one will call her a "baby" when she's offered a joint at the freshman dorms in the fall. Their eyes divulge a similar broader lust for future lofty adventures with vibrant and slightly sinister strangers. Yet in each other, they share no visions of lily-white porch swings upon which they sit hand-in-hand through decades of marital bliss. Instead, they recognize their immediate, necessary and identical needs to be primal, to exude wetness and scent; and to be thoroughly engaged in touch.

Within minutes of stepping through the front door, he turns her lackluster hello into a kiss that sops up the oils from her lips, cheeks, chin and neck. The tip of his tongue finally touches the tips of her eyelashes. Her breath warms the hollow of his throat and makes his Adam's apple quiver. The quickening of his pulse leads hers. She feels this hastening rhythm, not just in her chest, but steadily making itself known in the lower part of her belly and then even lower than there. The beat strengthens, forcing his hands to strip off the skirt and the loose top easily almost all in one motion. She wants this too, to feel solid and heavy and dripping with sweat. Suddenly she finds herself not returning his ardor. He is so busy moaning loudly, he doesn't notice her mood has changed. It is the emotionless start of the act that is too quick and too sudden, without her say or control that leaves her floating above and out of body.

 Losing lust, she finds that he is giving off a sickenly sweet odor, a mixture of too many store-bought scents, perhaps Old Spice, cheap pomade, cinnamon. But slowly, as if being led back to the floor of a grand ballroom to dance, he pulls her down from where she is observing. No longer ethereal notions, they, the act and the feelings have become palpable. She does not want to acknowledge it but his touch does create electricity. The lothario succeeds for a little while. She dances timidly and finds that she does want him to be where he has already been, but his selfish insistence to reach the goal line, his lack of skill and build-up of touch, pushes her spirit out again.

She is the clinician once more: studying him. Watching. He tries to succeed at his lovemaking like a peacock showing off its feathers, unaware that she is still unsure of him and of this performance that is about to begin. If he had let up for even a moment, she would have told him to stop and start over. She desperately wants them both to move to the inner natural rhythm that expresses their purity, not jump and go like caricatures he and their classmates mimic from bombarding advertisements and movies. She thinks to herself, "He is hiding himself behind exaggeration, not once listening to the language of our bodies or taking notice that my voice is stuck in my throat and wants to get out."

The first time he was inside, the pain was searing and surprising. She held onto the white couch cushions underneath hoping the pain would end the first minute he broke through the thin wall of flesh. But soon the movements became a strange natural kinetic-ism between the two: of her wound beginning to beg for its attacker to strike again and again. Before she could fully enjoy the new activity, she pushed him off and watched his mouth form an "o" underneath eyes full of surprise. "I thought you weren't a...." his whisper trailed off as a pool of blood soaked the fabric beneath her body.

After that night, he wanted to prove something in the bedroom, even if it had been in their friend's living room on a second hand couch. He wanted there to be some meaning to that night because she seemed to have taken it so lightly, was non-chalant about it and not needy afterwards. It didn't occur to him that she may have had ulterior motives for him. Perhaps that he had been her goal, an item to check off a list. In any case, he wanted to finish fully and thought she would be more of an equal player this time around. Now on the small bed in the room where she grew up, she is still hard to reach so he continues to try to give the situation a feeling he thinks every girl should want to have for a thing like this.

But she's not an every girl and though she notes he has a chiseled jaw line, brown popular boy eyes and a smooth rippling belly, she remains disengaged. He has a body made handsome from the many hours of football practice on the fields but with the technique of a self-absorbed naked molerat, blind to everything except his own needs. After another few minutes of her half-hearted pats on his broad back, he sees she's not looking at him at all and slows down. He seems to be annoyed with her for not being interested at all in their game. In moments, the lust falls away from his limbs and his eyes clear.

As he looks thoughtfully down at her, she is given a moment to breathe and assert herself. She whispers up to him, "I don't like to waste a visit, especially ones that have been pre-planned." It turns out, as soon as he stopped trying so hard without all the wheezing and pawing, she became fully aroused. She is now definitely in the mood to play. Her mind races to get his show of feathers back again. Before he can start to clothe himself, she pulls him towards her casually with just a hint of urgency.

She shifts her hips so they are square against and underneath his pelvis. The heat is still there where she knew it would be and like a fisherman, she throws out a hook by smiling and moves her fingers lightly across his damp skin. Her hands pull on his slick muscular arms and this time she doesn't mind the crescendoing moans, in fact she joins in.

She discovers she likes instigating and calling the shots. "Is this what it takes," she thinks. Must be... because his unctuous artificial smells have dissipated from her sensitive nose and she can truly smell him now. Their moist wet skin extends from the back of their ear lobes, along the sides of their necks down to the rim of their belly buttons and as he has pulled her underthings down and she has pushed all elastic waistbands off of him, the anticipation and excitement created by their equal and mutual excitement go off like July 4th sparklers that she can almost hear and see. He parts her legs by nudging her upper left thigh outwards with his knee. His fingertips help by brushing against the swollenness of her sex so that her right leg shivers and shifts outwards as well. She lunges up towards his half open mouth to engorge the opening with her hungry thrusting tongue. As soon as his eyes close to taste and savor the cavern of her mouth, he places his hands on her hips and taps once lightly against the swelling and pushes a penetration through so strongly she gasps, pulling air out of his lungs and causing her to grip his arms so hard they leave clear impressions of all her fingers. The pain is a shiver that goes from the top of her head down to her extremities, to the rounded tips of her nails, to the very ends of her long dark hair. But before she can even think about it, he has shifted and already begun to pull back, not even letting her gulp, while he is breathing harder satisfying his lust for her at an increasingly rapid tempo, making her pain mix with a maddening pleasure. She is the louder one at this juncture.

When she opens her eyes to look up at him, she sees small stabs of light all around as if they were both inside a small sun. Her heart is beating as fast as his. She has let go of the observant clinician and become the crass courtesan—guttural, exuding only sounds connected to his movements. He has finally found their rhythm. It continues to quicken and she feels she cannot get enough of him as she pushes against him thinking each stroke is deep but the next is deeper still. Rays of light feel as if they are shooting out of her fingers and ankles and toes as together, they reach a zenith and she is able to catch a breath while he wipes a sheen of sweat off his entire face. He pulls her to him and then gently rocks them both down to a simmering decrescendo. Finally, they land giggling softly to each other in a limpid pool of blissful juices and the smiles they give each other are genuine. The slow-down creates a soft spot in her heart. He is now a friend who just happens to be a lover, treating her with traditional post-coital tenderness.

Sighing and breathing shallowly lasts for a few minutes but he's the one who gets serious first. Pulses quicken once more and he kisses her for a long time, assumes a position and makes her complement it. He leaves with a final deep push as her eyes widen to accept it, indicating that she understands he wants no confusion about his role in all of this. She exhales deeply and then watches lazily as he jumps up to pull on his jeans, summer tee and running shoes. She rubs in the small soft peck on her forehead as she hears the Karmann Ghia sputter alive and do a soft peel out of the driveway. The second time went just the way she wanted it.

DAPHNE

By Lyndsey Ellis

When Daphne lost her baby, she cried like a wolf. A lone wolf, howling in darkness. She grew fur and claws. Black beaded eyes. Four triangular fangs. Her jaw line changed, transforming into a tube of a nose and mouth. Hands limp at her sides, she drew her head and torso back, held her face up to the sky and wailed strange things.

Someone slapped her. Dolores. Had to be Dolores. Daphne's screams faded to whimpers and eventually, she lost her voice but she remained with her lips open, hot air pumping ferociously up her lungs and out into the world.

Her knees buckled. She was down on all fours. Warm soil oozed between her toes. Coddled her spine. Crawled through her hair. Crashed into her cheek.

"It looks like....oh, what's that thing you used to play with when you were little? Mr. Potato Head! Good God."

Daphne's mother sipped her mango-flavored iced tea through a straw, her eyes fixed on Baby's head: a ball of plastic grocery bags stuffed into the leg of one of Daphne's old pantyhose. She wiped her mouth with the gym towel around her neck, wrung her hands together and let out one of her exaggerated sighs.

The duffel bag on the kitchen counter fell over. Its contents—MAC lip gloss, deodorant, a Redbook magazine, peppermints, gym membership card, loose change, iPod, and Black n' Milds—spilled out. Daphne watched her mother pull out a cigar from the 5-pack and trick it, a weary 'Don't ask' look engraved on her face.

Of all the women Daphne knew, Dolores was by far the most feminine. A whiff of dainty contempt bounced off of her everywhere she went. The Black n' Mild habit was a nasty joke, a weapon of irony. All the manners and lady-like refinement wrapped up into a single human being and then, as if to say 'Gotcha!', her mother pulled the rug from underneath the convinced.

"I thought you quit," Daphne said.

"So much for appearances," replied Dolores. "You know, you could've been a little bit choosier. Picked a doll with some clothes or all of its fingers or---."

"Open a window. Daddy'd shoot you dead if he knew."

"--at least one with a head."

"She *has* a head."

"*It* has a head. Maybe we should see about a doctor."

"Ah, a pediatrician."

Dolores grabbed Daphne's wrist.

"Just stop it. It's not right. You carrying on like this isn't natural."

Daphne let her wrist go limp and stared up at the ceiling, a habit she knew her moth-
er hated. But Dolores hated a lot of things: bare legs under dresses, tattoos on girls,
books exceeding 200 pages, refrigerator magnets, bad penmanship, purses with no
built-in mirrors, Aunt Bee's misshapen afro...

One of Daphne's favorites was her mother's low tolerance for drab meals. Since she
was a kid, she remembered Dolores laboring in the kitchen, the back of her blouse
stained with sweat, to come up with exquisite dishes that had to look just as physical-
ly appealing as they were healthy and delicious. Rainbow plates, Daphne called them.
At a time when watching Rainbow Brite, Punky Brewster and Care Bears came only
second to owning a Teddy Ruxpin, she didn't mind following her mother's food
etiquette. She even impressed her kindergarten teacher a few times when, during
playgroup, she arranged the other kids' play-dough on their plates from darkest to
lightest.

In the beginning, the change didn't start with food. Daphne didn't have an oppos-
ing thought about the color scheme. She just got older. Outgrew Rainbow Brite.
Accepted Punky Brewster's departure from television. Stashed her Care Bear collec-
tion in a corner underneath her bed.

By age twelve, color made her nauseous. The gothic age and the grunge revolution
both appealed to her and Daphne wound up mixing the two styles to suit her tastes,
making herself a spectacle to the hip-hop heads and the rock cliques. She was the
only black girl in her sixth grade class with a studded leash, uncombed hair, black
lipstick and an array of flannel shirts from the Salvation Army. While the other
black girls at school were donning Tommy Hilfiger threads, dooky braids and bob-
bing their heads to Tupac anthems, she was dreaming of moving to Seattle and elop-
ing with Kurt Cobain.

The unkempt locks caused the most friction between Daphne and her mother. She
often came home from school to hair accessories and shampoos planted in her
bathroom cabinet. Some colorful dress hidden in her heap of black clothing at
the bottom of her closet. Pages ripped from her Edgar Allen Poe and Sylvia Plath
collections and thrown all over her bedroom floor. Daphne uprooted the cream
carpet in her bedroom and painted the hardwood floor black, and Dolores ordered
her father to withhold her allowance 'until further notice.' She wasn't having sex
yet, or even thinking about it, but Daphne stole condoms from Aunt Bee's room in
the basement, used the rubbers for a science project at school, and placed the empty
wrappers in random areas around her room to make her mother crazy.

The two of them weren't on speaking terms when Daphne had her tonsillectomy
the next year. Nothing changed after the operation; Dolores's maternal instincts
failed to kick in and she didn't take Daphne to the doctor for the follow-up visit. As
the wedge between them grew, the only good thing for Daphne was finally having a
legitimate reason not to talk to her mother during the grueling recovery.

Daphne was confined to a diet of crushed ice and soft foods: pudding, oatmeal, ice
cream, mashed potatoes. Occasionally, her dad brought her fudge from the bakery

across from his office and once, she convinced herself she'd die if she didn't get her hands on Aunt Bee's leftover pound cake. Lots of ferocious gagging, a 2-hour stay at the ER and several painkillers later, she was glad to have gotten a flinch out of her mother.

The two finally exchanged words the following week. A Sunday. Her mother's birthday. Daphne remembered how the rain fell in sheets as they rode to the family's favorite restaurant. It would've been the perfect excuse to be covered in black but, by then, she was over her grunge-gothic days. She wanted a boyfriend and, befriending cheerleaders, she was determined to enter high school the next year as a girly girl. She saved the scraps of her father's allowance for trips to the nail shop when she and her friends ditched classes together. They wore almost any color, although pastels were still off limits.

The buffet house was beyond tempting and Daphne was glad she'd recuperated from the cake incident. With the exception of meat, bread and salad, she helped herself to almost everything at the buffet. She smacked her lips and kept one eye open on her plate as her father said grace.

"That plate's not colorful enough," her mother said over the mumbled chorus of Amen's. She pointed at Daphne's plate. "It's missing warmth. Something red, brown, or orange. Maybe some yellow."

Daphne didn't consider anything; it was second nature. She harked and gathered the biggest wad of saliva from the base of her raw throat, exerted a marbled ball of spit— fresh blood, coagulated brown gunk, mucus the color of a pumpkin--between the potatoes and spinach on her plate.

She looked into her mother's eyes, Auntie Bee pounding the table with her manly fist in admiration and her father, fiddling with his pager.

"Dolores."

Daphne said her mother's name but she didn't hear herself. She assumed her mother hadn't heard her either, until her berry red nails loosened around Daphne's wrist. Finally, Dolores released her, lit the cigar and took a drag. The overwhelming sweet smell was usually sickening. Now, it was barely noticeable and almost pleasant.

"Dolores," Daphne repeated. She took away the cigar, pretended to smoke it, sashayed to the center of the kitchen, swirled and curtsied. The breeze she picked up felt good between her toes and on the patch of skin above her elbow where Baby rested her head. She felt like she was 9 years old again, stepping foot onto the church's outside steps with her eyes closed, waiting giddily for a light wind to tickle the places where she'd gathered the most sweat: her underarms, the backs of her knees, the crevice between her father's colossal hand and her stick-like fingers. Especially, between the tiny openings of those sweltering stockings Dolores made her wear regardless of the temperature because bare legs under skirts was the gateway to whoredom.

Daphne eyed Baby. Fingered a thin tear that began in the back of her head. Finally, the stockings had served a purpose. A better one than what her mother had intended. And now Daphne, too, had developed her own sense of irony, her own 'Gotcha!' to the convinced.

"Monty called again this morning." Dolores ran a hand through her cropped hair. "I take it you two haven't talked."

"You take it right."

"He sounded terrible."

"The fool won't wear shoes or underwear."

"Hush. I'm not talking about the common cold." She motioned for Daphne to return her cigar.

Daphne took her time getting over to the counter. Watched her mother's manicured hand shake as she held it out. The standard inevitable also applied to Dolores. This silly woman Daphne went through pains to love was getting old. A heavy warmth blanketed her face and she blinked back the blurriness, recalling the same hand parting the hair on her head down the middle, deftly but delicately. As Dolores applied pressure, Daphne felt like her scalp was being sliced open. She sat on her fingers and squirmed until she was told for the umpteenth time to 'Hold still, tenderheadedness come with a cost.' The tips of Dolores's fingers—berry red then, too, but with more length to the nail—swept past her eye as they gathered a hunk of hair, clumped it together with a rubber band, plaited it, even smoothed down her widow's peak before Daphne could finish protesting, "But Mama, I thought you said it was hardheadedness that came with a cost."

Slap!

There was always a slap. Then, "be still." Or "hold it." "Don't move." "Hush." But Dolores never saw results. Didn't get the things she'd always asked of Daphne all those years. Before the accident, it had taken a long time for her not to cry, not to talk, not to move, to just be still. Daphne willed herself to be still from the moment she woke up in her sister's bed after the funeral and lay there listening to folks chatter, the dishes clinking downstairs with Luther Vandross's *Give Me the Reason* hovering in the background. Licking a thick coat of mucus off her front teeth and feeling her eyelids swell under hunks of crust that hung from her lashes. She couldn't think. Her mind was a chasm and she was so still, hoping and praying from the pocket of her soul that her body would take the hint and catch up. Give out, free itself and dissolve.

Soon, she was on her way. Her bones became loose and brittle. Her joints ached and she smelled her own stink. There were times when she couldn't tell if she was just waking up or just falling asleep. Dolores would be saying something to her—talking close enough for her lips to touch her ear—and she sounded like she was calling to her through the other end of a cave.

One day, Dolores was reading the funnies to Daphne on the front porch one morning after breakfast. Her father had her propped up in one of the rocking chairs before he left for work so that she'd be able to face her mother and look at the newspaper's illustrations. Dolores interrupted herself and laughed aloud at something she'd read. Daphne hadn't heard the punch line, but she watched her mother throw her head back, the bulges in her tight-fitting blouse vibrating as she exploded in cackles. Then, the paper was on the ground and those berry nails were upside Daphne's face.

"You think you in hot shit, dontcha?"

Dolores's propriety fell away from her voice, the years of a shameful upbringing in the slums pouring out in its place. Dolores didn't curse; she didn't believe in it. She looked like she'd seen the devil.

"Before you, I had five miscarriages, *five*," she continued, "and this act you got goin' was old news to me after the second one. This stops now, ya hear me? Ends right here. Or I'll kill you myself."

That night, Aunt Bee laughed in Daphne's face as she bathed her. It was the first time Daphne had opened her mouth since the burial. Her voice was croaky and her breath foul. Her words were slurred through teeth that felt weak enough to crumble.

"Five miscarriages? *Shee-yit...*" Aunt Bee waved it off. "That ain't even possible. Your mama had abortions, girl. Two of 'em."

She laughed with Aunt Bee and cried on her lap, relieved to feel in herself again. Paced her room all night, singing to a pillow in her bosom. An image of her sister, little Danika, in her mind and how she'd watched Daphne rouse from a choppy sleep in her bed the morning after the repass. Bouncing on her tip-toes and picking the skin off her chapped lips. The front of her jumper tucked deep into her tights. A headless baby doll in the crook of her arm, its caramel rubbery body bare and sooty with permanent marker scribblings across the limbs and protruding belly.

"Go back to him, Daphne," Dolores was saying. "Stop being selfish. Get through this together. Imagine what would happen if he saw you like this."

"Daddy put you up to this, didn't he?"

Dolores didn't answer. She took another long drag and glowered at Daphne through the white haze that came out of her mouth.

"You should start coming to the gym with me. You're face is getting fat."

"It's called bloating. I'm on the rag," Daphne blurted.

"Honey, don't say that. It's such an ugly phrase. The filth that comes out of your mouth sometimes."

"Is this about getting me out the house? If you want me out, I'm out."

"Well, it's not the first time you dragged yourself back here. Hush now and call him. And give that, that *thing*, back to your sister..."

Dolores held out the cordless phone over the kitchen's island. The skin between her eyes broke into wrinkles and she fixed her brows into a sympathetic arch, her hand shaking like it was prepared to disband from her wrist.

Daphne slid into her sandals and pulled Baby into her. She snatched the Black n' Mild from her mother again, dropped it in the sink, turned on the faucet and marched out the side door.

She sat Indian-styled with hair that fell past her shoulders. It was healthier than she remembered, thick as she'd always wanted it to be. It hung effortlessly and swayed from side to side. *Whoosh. Whoosh.*

Berry red finger tips caught it in one snatch. Dolores's knees firmly held her in place. She held the hair up high, brought it back down, smiled sweetly and said something over her shoulder to her own mother.

Grandmother stood, nodding her response and added a colorless ribbon to Dolores's braid. Silver ringlets cascaded down her back. Looked like an aluminum waterfall. So shiny and overflowing that the muscles in her neck hurt from straining to find where grandmother's curls ended. She wanted to rub them but her hands weren't free. They were bound around what felt like the beginnings of a braid. A wet one. Smooth and slippery with snapping, rubbery sounds coming from its mattedness as she tried to grip the three divided sections between her fingers. Only super clean hair did that. She beamed. Turned around to face the pretty locks and found braided worms rooted in tar black soil.

She woke up pulling at her fingers, her nipples bleeding fresh milk.

RAINBOW ROSES

By Anne Lynch

The porch door sprung shut and the wood banged a few times until the door came to a resting place in its frame. Virginia Sutherland grasped the thin metal railing to steady herself as she walked slowly down the steps to her late husband's rose garden. She carried her pruning equipment in a thick plastic purse, which bore the face of Leonardo DiCaprio as a teenager. She had picked it up at a yard sale years ago and it tickled her to death.

Virginia made a point of picking up her feet each time she stepped and was also careful not to dirty her dark pink Converses. Her doctor told her she was starting to shuffle in her old age and to beware of the infamous "Hip Replacement Shuffle." When she was younger she was baffled by the numbers of seniors at her church on the prayer list for hip replacement and now somehow the years had flown by and she was in the seniors club at church. At least her doctor had a sense of humor and she laughed to herself every time she picked up her feet.

Her Converse shoes were a gift from her daughter Shelley referencing the multitude of colors Shelley had collected in high school. Thirty some years ago Virginia joked that Shelley wouldn't stop until she had every color in the rainbow. Now Virginia scoffed at rainbows. She couldn't even look at a real one in the sky without thinking about her daughter and her lesbian lady friend. It seemed that the gays wanted to take over everything and couldn't even leave the rainbow alone. She almost didn't want to wear the shoes. She thought Shelley was putting the whole gay thing in her face again. There was also a good chance that she was overreacting. Shelley had gone out of her way to put in orthopedic inserts and she rarely gave her anything at all. A gift was a gift and one from her daughter had a way of touching a chord.

Way back when on May 23rd, 1933, not that she is keeping track, Virginia caught Shelley French kissing another girl at a sleepover. It was terrible. The girls had been up giggling all night and Virginia could see the flashlights from the crack under the door. Virginia was in the sitting room crocheting a throw and it got quiet. Then there was a little squeal and then a muffled giggle. And then a sigh. The type of sigh that should only come from a parent's bedroom late at night when the children are deep asleep and dreaming. Virginia knew that sigh and couldn't fathom why it was coming from her fourteen year old's bedroom. Virginia put aside her throw and walked right into Shelley's room without knocking. The girls were intertwined and she couldn't see where her daughter ended and the other girl began. All she saw was their mouths glued together and thank god she never saw where there hands were.

Her name was Allison. She was a hussy and she ruined Virginia's life. She was from the wrong side of the tracks and Virginia should have never let them become friends in the first place. Of course, that sleepover was Shelley's last sleepover. And her last week in public school. And her first week at the Christian Academy. Virginia was ready to do anything and everything to put her daughter back on the right path. In fact, she had always been hesitant about putting her daughter in public schools, but Walter had assured her that they were good. That they were safe. Safe my pewtutie she thought.

Virginia lowered herself down on the wooden bench in the middle of the garden. Funny how one memory can trigger the next and before you know it you're back there. Today she sat on Walter's side and put her bag of tools on her side. She tried to imagine what it would have been like to be the man she devoted her entire life to. Walter was calm and fair and loved to be outside with his hands in the dirt and he didn't give a god damn whether his only daughter ever got married to a man or had children. Shelley could have run off to the circus and he would have been front and center cheering her on. He would have even paid for her to go to clown school. Anything for his baby girl.

Virginia slowly pushed herself up off the bench and got out her pruners. Too much thinking got her down plus she had work to do. She hadn't been out back all month and the roses needed some help. She started by walking the entire garden to get a scope of what lay ahead of her. Right next to the bench were the Mr. Lincolns.

"Why hello, Mr. President," Virginia said to the rose bush as if Abe Lincoln was there instead. "How are you today?" She paused as if listening to his answer and added, "Why thank you, I am doing very well." She bent down closer to a large red rose and let it rest in her hand while she inhaled the aroma slowly. She looked at the rose lovingly and added, "Did you know we have a black president these days? Yes, sir. We do. Yes, I did vote for him, yes I did."

Virginia let go of the rose and snipped the uppermost thorns off one at a time. Her head jerked back suddenly and she dropped her arms down to her side. "I most certainly did not think she had any business running for vice president. Did you!? For all I care she can stay up there in Alaska with the grizzly bears where she belongs."

Next on the brick pathway were her Anabells. They were a coral orange and clustered together in what was called Floribunda. She picked three for her kitchen table and slid them in her Leonardo bag.

Anabell's neighbor was Gertrude Jekyll. Virginia was fond of calling this bush Aunt Gertrude. Gertrude's tight pink flowers did not like the company of other roses and Virginia found herself shaking her head at the bush and saying, "Ornery."

Virginia cut two for her vase and put them beside the Anabells in her bag. Anabell was inching over into Aunt Gertrude's space and Virginia thought it was about time to transplant her ornery aunt. A tree had fallen in last winter's snowstorm and opened up the canopy on the other side of the garden. There was finally enough light over there now to grow roses so Virginia decided she would call the neighbor boy to transplant the bush.

As Virginia walked a slight breeze made her hair shift ever so slightly. Her hairdresser had done a tighter perm than usual and she enjoyed the change. These days everything seemed the same. She woke up everyday and fixed her oatmeal in the microwave. She ate it slowly at the breakfast room table and picked her way through the local advertisements that came with the mail every Tuesday.

Once her mail lady had told her that mail carriers were just reverse garbage men. They delivered the trash every day and the garbage men picked it up once a week. Virginia agreed, but she liked the comfort that she was guaranteed at least one visitor a day. Her mail lady's name was Kristen. She was a sweet young girl and very talkative. And a quick talker at that. She loved to tell Kristen that she should work on the weekends as an auctioneer.

After her oatmeal, Virginia would set the bowl in her sink and run some water over it. Then she would put some water in her favorite mug. It was a large cream-colored mug that she bought at the Decatur Arts Festival. A woman that studied pottery at Callonwalde sold it to her for $18.00. At the time she almost didn't purchase it. Who ever heard of paying $18.00 for a coffee mug? But she kept staring at the ridges that seemed to flow perfectly along the sides of the mug so she had to have it.

Every morning Virginia would microwave her water for two minutes and drop in her green tea bag. Then she would drink her tea on the side porch. It was screened in and she could sit near the front of the house and wait for Kristen to bring the mail. Or she could sit facing the back of the house and look out at her husband's rose garden. Her life had evolved into a whole lot of sitting by herself and waiting for something to happen.

Virginia was glad to be out in the garden today. It made her blood move and it made her memories come alive. Mostly they were good ones. Ones of her and Walter talking in the garden. Holding hands. Even in their old age their wrinkly hands would grasp each others. Blue veins had appeared over the years and Walter would tell her that they were just absolutely beautiful and that he wasn't sure how he ever loved her before her veins surfaced. Others memories were not so good. Ones where Walter talked to Shelley in the garden and she was excluded. She could still see him wiping tears from their daughter's eyes.

In families there is always a good cop and a bad cop. Someone had to be the bad cop and it was her. Virginia turned back around to look at the bench and yelled, "Was I wrong to want a normal life for my daughter? What she's doing just isn't right." Virginia inhaled and when she exhaled the tears came rolling down her cheeks. "Why did you leave me so soon, Walter? You know I can't live without you."

Virginia could barely see with the tears streaming down her weathered face. She dropped her head to her chest and began shuffling back to the house. She needed to sell the damn thing. It was all just too much for her these days. Everything was just piling up on her heart and in her head and she didn't know how to find her way out. As she neared the stairs she looked back over her shoulder to see where she had come from and without warning her right ankle gave way and she began to fall to the ground in slow motion. Her right elbow missed the brick walkway and hit the dirt and her head fell down under Mr. Lincoln. Her Leonardo bag fell on top of her and thank heavens she didn't stab herself in the heart with the pruners. What an embarrassing way to die.

Virginia lay in shock for a few moments before letting out a loud yell. "Help! Help!" She looked up at the sky and imagined what it would be like if these were the last clouds she would ever see. One almost looked like a heart and then when she looked again it was gone. Another cloud looked like a walker and she shook her head knowing that she had just seen the future.

Virginia inhaled and began again. "I hope someone's listening because this is my big chance." In a louder voice she screamed out, "Help! I've fallen and I can't get up!" Silence. Virginia laughed to herself as she pulled a leaf out of her perm. How could she have possibly gotten to where she was? And why didn't she have the portable phone in her bag? She let out a few more helps and then reached for a Gertrude Jekyll in her bag. She pulled the coral petals off one at a time while she said, "Someone loves me. They love me not. Someone loves me. They love me not. Help! Someone loves me. Help! They love me not."

Virginia closed her eyes and listened to the birds chirping happily in the yard. Life goes on she thought. She wondered if she could make it through the night if no one ever came. And what if no one came tomorrow either? She could really die out here all crumpled on the ground like a garbage bag. She took another deep breath. "Help!"

At the hospital Virginia was told the inevitable: she needed hip replacement surgery. And when her daughter arrived her fate worsened. Shelley and her lady friend Carol had arranged a room for her in the old folks home they managed. Going to an old folks home would be bad enough, but the one they run was for old gays and lesbians. She would have never believed such a place existed in the South if her daughter hadn't been at the helm of it all. San Francisco maybe, but Atlanta no.

Shelley and Carol stood at her bedside and Shelley took Virginia's hand. With their matching company polo shirts on they almost looked like sisters. One woman just a shade darker than the other. Virginia looked up at her daughter and said, "I'm sorry you had to leave work to come over here."

Shelley squeezed her hand tighter and asked, "Are you ok?"

"If you call being laid up in the hospital with your rear end flopping in the wind ok, then yes. I'm ok."

Shelley's partner Carol laughed and said, "Well you must not be too bad off if you're still cracking jokes, Mom."

"I am not cracking jokes," Virginia said, "And for the last time I am not your Mom."

Carol turned to leave and whispered in Shelley's ear, "She fine. Still fired up and angry as always. See you back at The Rainbow." She patted Shelley on the behind and left the room.

"We've reserved a room for you at The Rainbow," Shelley said.

"The doctor told me. But since I'm not a leprechaun, nor am I a lesbian, I don't think there will be any room for me at the inn."

Shelley put her hand down gently and said, "After your hip replacement surgery, which by the way will be in the morning, you need 8 weeks to recover. You don't have to tell anyone at The Rainbow that you're a heterosexual. We operate on a strict don't ask don't tell policy. I've already called over to your church and they've put you on the prayer list and all that good stuff. I'll see you when you get out of surgery, Mom, and then when they discharge you I'll be here with the company van." Shelley bent over and kissed her mother on the forehead and walked out of the room. Virginia squeezed her eyes shut and tried to stop the tears from coming.

If it weren't for the fact that she was in a wheelchair you would of never been able to get Virginia through the doors of The Rainbow. This morning, however, her daughter pushed her right up to the glass doors and when they opened automatically she rolled Virginia through. Carol was right behind them and before Virginia could come to terms with reality a young man got up from behind the desk and rushed over to her. He bent down and gave her a kiss on each cheek and held her face in his hands. Shelley and Carol instinctively took a step back.

"Virginia!" he exclaimed, "Welcome to the Rainbow! My name is David and I'll be your cruise ship director. Of course there won't be a cruise, but I promise you, you are going to have the most amazing experience here and you'll never ever want to go home! We have so much fun and everyone is super sassy and interesting and you'll just absolutely love it!" David stood up and smiled from ear to ear.

"Young man," Virginia started. Carol and Shelley looked at each other and took a second step back. "I appreciate your enthusiasm, but I refuse to love it. If my mother was alive to see me now . . . being wheeled into a . . . a . . . a lesbian and gay facility like an old lady with one hip already in the grave. Well she'd push me in all the way so I could just get it over with."

Shelley tried to get David's attention by waving her hand, but he was looking straight at Virginia. "Please excuse our mother," Shelley said.

Virginia turned her head around towards Shelley. "Your mother. I did not birth Carol through my vagina."

Carol walked past Virginia and said, "You're very welcome, Mrs. Sutherland. I'm so happy that you'll be staying with us."

David ignored the tension and kept smiling. "Nothing to apologize about Shelley. Virginia, you will fit right in! You'll be ordering a personalized bingo caddy online before you even know it. Let me guess, you're a Braves Fan? Or maybe Phantom of the Opera? And if you don't mind me saying, I love the fact that you used the word vagina within your first five minutes at The Rainbow. I just love it! Welcome!"

Virginia lay in bed staring at the ceiling. There was a quiet knock on the door and before she could even say, "Come in," or "I'm in my skivvies, don't you open that door!" a stocky nurse in light blue scrubs entered the room and walked to Virginia's bed.

The nurse yawned and asked, "Do you need help to the bathroom?"

Virginia looked the nurse up and down. "What's your name young man?"

"Jennifer."

"I'm sorry, Dear. I've just never met a woman with such short hair. My daughter has short hair, but you're practically bald. Have you thought about a wig?"

The nurse headed back to the door. "Goodnight, Ma'am."

Virginia wanted to ask her to bring the telephone closer, but before she could Jennifer had already closed the door. Virginia detested those old lady hospital buttons and would much rather phone the nurses station if she needed help.

Virginia looked back at the ceiling and over at the phone on her rolling bedside table and then back at the door. She knew she was on her own and that the man-woman-nurse-person wasn't coming back. She stretched out her arm as far as she could and grasped on to the cord in effort to pull the phone and table towards her. The table wouldn't budge. She gave it a yank, hoping that the majority of the phone would fall unto the edge of her bed, but her hope sent the phone crashing to the floor. She sighed and pulled her quilt up to shoulders resigning herself to sleep. Before she could even shut her eyes the phone began beeping loudly.

"Damn it all to hell!" Virginia yelled, "Help!"

The phone continued to beep. It sounded like a Canadian goose with its head stuck in an echo chamber. Virginia scanned the room trying to determine how old the building was and what the chances were of the walls being thin enough for someone to hear the beeping and come make it stop. It felt like two minutes had passed and no one had rushed in. It was just a constant throbbing in her ear as the phone kept on beeping as if it could beep for 100 years and then beep another 100 more.

Virginia took a deep breath and yelled as loud as her tired lungs would allow. "Will someone pick that damn phone off the floor and turn it off for God's sakes!?" No response. Virginia sighed and pressed the red call button on her bed.

Jennifer responded through an intercom system on the wall behind Virginia's bed. "Nurses' station, this is Jennifer."

"Will someone pick my damn phone off the floor and turn it off for God's sakes?" Jennifer wasn't responding quick enough. Virginia took a deep breath and said, "Announcing a sale on garden supplies and home improvement merchandise! Announcing a sale! Hello gays and lesbians! The rainbow is disappearing! Hurry quick! If you don't put my phone back on the hook within the next thirty seconds the leprechauns will never let you put a rainbow on anything again! They want their rainbows back!"

A small crowd of Rainbow Residents had formed outside the nurse's station. They looked at each other in disbelief, but couldn't help but laugh. They covered each other's mouths so that their laughter couldn't be heard above the beeping of the phone. Winny had rolled up with her wheelchair and had even put down her cross-stitch in anticipation of what was to come next. Bruce came on his walker. He parked it at the wall and waved his partner Jeremiah to hurry up. Even the nutritionist Sybille sent a text to the groundskeeper Jimmy to join them.

Now Virginia started imitating the phone with frightening accuracy. Her loud beeping in unison with the phone triggered scoring from the group. They started holding up their fingers for points. Most people gave her eight fingers and she even got a nine from Jeremiah. Stuart wanted to give her a ten, but was locked into an eight due to the two missing fingers on his left hand. To most everyone's disappointment, her performance was interrupted when Jimmy arrived with Shelley. Before Shelley even got the chance Jimmy walked over to the nurse's intercom and flicked the off switch.

Shelley took a deep breath and motioned the gawkers away and took off down the hall to her mother's room. Shelley always wished her mother's sharp mind had been put to better use. That she had been born in a different generation where a woman wasn't only expected to pop out babies and cook three hot meals a day. She could

have been the president of a large corporation. She had no problem giving direc-
tions, that's for sure.

"Mother!" Shelley said, "What is going on in here? Everyone on the hall can hear you
hollering and screaming and beeping and everything in between."

"I knew y'all could hear me and just like when I fell at home, no one came. That
seems to be a theme. Left out to dry. The lone ranger. The last Eskimo. The old
spinster with her cats. And I don't even have any cats. It's just me."

"Are you finished?" Shelley asked.

"Will you please pick up that damn phone and shut it up? Or better yet, hand it to
me and I will throw it out the damn window into that shallow pond out there. That
pond doesn't even have enough water in it for a decent man to be able to drown him-
self if he so pleases."

Shelley shook her head and stooped down to pick up the phone. She placed it back
on the receiver and let the silence overpower the room. She counted to herself. One,
two, three, four, five, six, seven. It was a game she played as a child. How long can
her mother remain in silence without opening her mouth? Eight, nine . . .

"God Bless America, I can hear myself think again."

Shelly walked back towards the door. As she left, she let out a faint, "Goodnight,
Mom," and then shut the door behind her.

The next day, Nurse Jennifer pushed Virginia down the hall in a squeaky wheelchair.
Other residents tried to greet her, but she kept her head down. For once in her life
she found herself quiet and it was difficult for her. She tried to concentrate on the
sound of the chair and when that failed she began making a mental list of the pos-
sessions she could sell to afford to pay for hip rehab somewhere else. The lump sum
she was told was about $100,000. How could she have been so stupid to fall in her
garden? If only the real Leonardo DiCaprio had been there having tea with her on
not just on her bag. He would have saved her.

What could she sell she wondered. There was her parent's grandfather clock. Maybe
she could get $1,000 for it. The last time it chimed was the day her husband had
died. It was the weirdest thing. When she inherited the clock it hadn't worked in
years and Walter was always begging her to let him get it fixed. She didn't care much
for the constant bonging as a child so she never called the repairman. Walter died
in the hospital with her and Shelley at his side and when her church friend drove her
home she went straight for the bed. She was ready to collapse from exhaustion and
as she passed the grandfather clock it chimed three times. It was her Walter saying
goodbye.

She could sell her piano, but it wasn't anything special. From what she knew people
were in line at her church to be able to donate their pianos. It might even cost more
to get rid of it than to keep it. She also had some costume jewelry. Maybe one or two
pieces held some value. There was a broach from way back when. It was gold looking,
but not real gold, and it had the figure of a dancing woman. She was wearing a long
skirt and Virginia never could decide if she was holding flowers in the air or a torch
of some kind.

Her house was furnished in a modest manner and the only thing worth anything was only worth something to her. She wasn't even sure she could sell the house for over $200,000. It had a good size to it. It was four bedrooms, two baths. But it didn't have any fancy upgrades like her neighbors had made over the years. There was no sunroom or skylights and there was not a California closet to speak of. The basement was a basement, not a bonus room. And the appliances and fixtures were original. Maybe she could sell it to a young couple who were retro or vintage or old school or whatever they call it. Or maybe a vegetarian. Do vegetarians want all the thrills in life? No. They don't. If they did they would eat beef and pork and veal and duck. Nothing, but the best. Or she thought, maybe for economic purposes only she would consent to sell it to a gay. Or two gays. They always seem to love to fix things up.

But from the looks of things the gays haven't been put in charge of decorating at The Rainbow. Most of the floors were linoleum; where there was carpet, it was worn thin. The pattern had long since faded into a light green blob. The walls were painted light yellow and the artwork was less than mediocre. It looked like it had been purchased at a thrift store. No theme could be detected. At least not by Virginia. Some were still-lifes. Some were landscapes. And then the occasional portrait. Who knew who the portraits were of and what that person might think if they knew their face was up on these walls. That was the weird thing about art. Once it was sold the artist had no control of where it ended up. And the person in the picture had even less.

"Who is in charge of decorating?" Virginia blurted out despite her vow to keep her mouth shut.

"Not me," Jennifer replied, "I don't much care for the style of these pieces."

"Who would care for them? They're atrocious. They sap the life right out of you."

"Someone must have thought they looked nice," Jennifer said as her eyes glanced over the art for the first time in months. "To tell the truth Mrs. Sutherland, I never gave it much thought."

"I think someone needs to do something about it," Virginia said.

"If there was money, I'm sure it would have been done already."

"Well, then they need to stop wasting money on putting me up," Virginia said.

"I mentioned that," Jennifer replied.

Virginia pushed the hand brakes down and the wheelchair jerked to a stop. "Excuse me? You mentioned what? I am your customer. You don't get to say whether I stay or go. I get to say whether I stay or go. Do you understand me?"

Jennifer bent down and released the brakes. She rolled Virginia into the elevator and reached her hand inside to press the ground floor button. The doors closed behind Virginia and she found herself alone and staring at the wall. There was a flyer for an art class later that day. It read, "Paper Flower Making for Beginners." The doors opened and Virginia could hear the other residents behind her walking to lunch. She reached down to try to wheel herself out of the elevator, but she wasn't fast enough. The door binged closed again and the elevator started its way back up.

[expletive deleted]

By Nana K. Twumasi

to the person who called me a nigger on saturday night:

you said it so casually, as though you say it all the time. you cruised by and shouted, "hey, nigger!" out of your car window, and there was laughter on the edge of your tongue, so perhaps i mistook your intended affection for vitriol. but you didn't say, "hey, nigga," that pronunciation being the friendly, colloquial use of the word, and while i don't personally approve of it, i understand that it's possible that you toss the word around with the two sort-of-black, sort-of-friends you might have and while i can't speak for the entire black race, neither of those uses are acceptable to me. but you didn't say "nigga," or even, "my nigguh," both being nice ways of casually dropping a pejorative; you said "nigger," and you laughed, and sped on, like it was nothing.

you seemed young, so perhaps you're not aware of the long, sordid history that word drags with it. basically, the word nigger means "black." of course you must have some idea of that since you directed it specifically at me and not the two caucasian people i was with—clearly, you have some modicum of intelligence. if you break it down, the word originates from the spanish/portugese "negro," which in turn comes from latin, "niger," which also, as it must be obvious to you now, means "black." i hope you're following this—i know the study of latin hasn't been part of standardized curriculum for a long while, and i'd guess that you missed the vocabulary lesson that makes it clear it is easy to uncover a word's meaning if you can find its latin roots. so now we understand that the word "nigger," at some point in history, meant "black." that's harmless enough. i'm sure you learned that, for a few hundred years, persons of my color worked against their will in the service of persons of your color—this was called slavery. every country who maintained the peculiar institution of slavery has apologized for it, but it's possible your ancestors were not among the repentant. taking all that into account, it should be evident that not only did the word nigger mean "black," it was also used to identify someone of inferior intelligence, barely human, incapable of learning to any wide degree, gainfully participating in society, or making choices for his or herself.

so basically you called me an ignorant person of african descent.

i'll admit i am two of those things: a person, and of african descent, but i imagine it's now wildly obvious that i am not ignorant. however, i can still assume with the best of them. so i'll assume that you, riding in the passenger seat of your friend's beat up honda civic, and not the cool kind, rather, a cast-off, boxy late eighties model that his parents gave to him, quite likely live in your own parent's basement. you were wearing a white baseball cap backwards on your fat pasty head and i'm guessing the cap said something clever over the bill; maybe you bought a "U. MASS"

hat and removed the "M" so it says, "U. ASS." how naughty of you. whiteboys like
you love nonsense like that, right? you were out of shape and you had a thin stain
of a moustache clinging to your sweaty upper-lip, so i'll gather that you haven't had
sex since you were seventeen, and it had to have been a mercy-fuck from the dowdy,
pimple-faced girl who settled for you just that one time, because even she knew she
could do better, one day.

the thing is, i don't really have a comeback that would adequately match, in baseless-
ness or brevity. i can't call you "cracker"; historically, the word originally referred
to the white slave driver who would "crack the whip." so that's not really an insult.
in fact, you might find it empowering. i could try "honky," but honestly, that's not
really very derogatory since no one seems to know where it comes from. "whitey?"
too simple and not enough oomph. "redneck?" because that term theoretically
defines someone who has put in a hard day's worth of manual labor such that the
back of his neck had been reddened by the sun (and sure, as long as we're making
unfair assumptions, perhaps he has a couch on his porch and the skeleton of a car in
his unpaved driveway—but so what?), it's not fitting for you since your doughy arms,
glassy eyes and slack jaw made evident to me that you haven't done a day of honest
work in your life.

you not only insulted me, and very nearly made me cry, you also reminded me, as
so many of those of your kind have, that there is no sufficient way to offend a white
person. but you don't really care about all that. you just let the word go and you
and your equally unattractive friend had a nice laugh about it and then you prob-
ably drove up on some girls who were leaving the club and cat-called them to prove
you were men, since being a man automatically gives you the right to make sugges-
tive, aggressive, comments about any woman who has the misfortune of crossing
your path. then you went home and maybe played video games in the dank basement
i want you to live in and, maybe you thought about all the hot girls you saw, and
brushed away the thought that you hadn't touched any one of them. and surely, you
thought about the unsuspecting girl who you called a nigger, and how she stopped
in mid-step and screwed up her face; how she might have thrown something at you
if she'd had anything other than her purse. and how it doesn't really matter that,
in all counts, she is legitimately better than you, or that the history of slavery is not
one she can honestly claim as it was given to her only as a consequence of the place
she grew up but is not really part of her history, or that she's existed for many years
confronting other people's assumptions about how people should behave, based on
the way they look.

no. you just laughed, and drove away, leaving me holding the bag.

how can you write

By Jason Kolbrich

how can you write

when the list of endeavors grows another thousand things long that you'll finish the day they're due

and that just won't do

but you need more time and that only works out when you're out of work and you can't pay the rent like that

but every now and again you can scrape enough together to buy a bottle of cheap red wine that just complicates your relationship with your girlfriend

who's really a woman but no one says 'womanfriend'

and the wine tries to break through the stone wall around the fortress of yourself but it only stains the mortar

which cripples you with enough

lucidity stupidity debility

to search for more wine or something a little harder to take away the pain

that you now think you harbor — and your roommate's small bottle of vodka in the freezer from his last big party will do just fine

there's nothing to mix it with but hell go on you're a man mixers are for wimps and writers are tough

and in all the classes you've had you've always heard how all writers have to have a vice and this one will do for the moment

it's not illegal or very expensive and besides your roommate would understand

you'll replace it later when your student loan check arrives next semester

so the icicle-like sting twitches down to join the bottle of red wine in your stomach

and one whole hour and half a bottle later the fortress seems more like a sand castle getting washed away with the tide of 80 proof clear as crystal Russian vodka

and nothing seems as important as getting that old tape your ex-girlfriend made you and playing it on the boom-box your present (but absent) girlfriend got you for your birthday last month

and you wonder what she (your ex-) is doing right now — which will expand into an ocean of dreams — and as you sink beneath those waves you call and ask her if she wants to come over and just talk because no one really seems to listen any more

and she was so good at listening to you — like you were the only person in the world

and no — you're not going out with anyone right now — no no one could ever hold a candle to her brilliance

— you don't know why you stopped going out either

— you miss her too

and when you open the door she will hug you hello and talk about everything and nothing until a cliché silence breaks up more than just the tension

when you wake up you remember the paper you should have been working on — and your ex-girlfriend will roll over and give you a kiss and her essay from a semester ago

which you turn in as your own work — and you make sure to pick up the paper as soon it's graded so the teacher won't have it around to compare

but now still drunk with the limerence of last night you will stumble through a goodbye and a tear will run down your cheek

which your ex- will misinterpret as a sign that you don't want her to go and that you still love her

and this reminds you that you have a girlfriend which makes you cry more and your ex- kisses away the pain and you fall in bed all over again

the same bed that you used to share with the girl that is your new ex.

who will find out about this little indiscretion (your term) and slap that same tear filled cheek but no tears will come and that fact alone will make her hit you again only harder

but the only thing that you can think about is that paper

because this is only a slap on the face not like getting expelled for plagiarism

but later you will think it's cool to say that you passed the class but lost your girl-friend

MODERATION

By Jason Kolbrich

René holds her mug by the rim and swirls the last gulp of coffee around before she drinks it. "You know the problem won't fix itself."

Chuck looks around his kitchen and back to his empty plate on the table. "But all I said was that I wanted to try and figure out something to do with all those fragments I have."

"Don't you understand, that's symptomatic."

"What do you mean, it's symptomatic?" He looks from the crumbs on his plate to René's green eyes.

René glances from side to side, as if they were in a crowded café and not Chuck's kitchen. She leans across the table and whispers; "You don't know what 'symptomatic' means?"

He sits back in his chair and watches René cross her legs, half hidden by the table. "I do. I just thought…I just thought that. Well, you know, if I can't make-up an ending, there might be something else I could do with what I've already written."

"But that's symptomatic!" René shakes her head no and her long red curls follow. "Urrgghh! It doesn't solve the problem of not finishing the stories. Does it? All you're doing is making it so you don't have to write any endings. Why don't you try and figure out why you can't create an ending? Don't you understand what I mean?"

"But it's not a problem."

"Yes, it is. We had this discussion last semester, when you told about the idea: You can't write a story made up of just beginnings and middles."

"I could try."

"But it wouldn't be a story! What the hell is wrong with you? Haven't you learned anything as a creative writing major? I've only had one class but I still know about conflict introduction and resolution. What's that crap; rising action, climax, falling action? You were the t. a. remember?"

"It's not crap." whispers Chuck.

"To you it is, if you want to write a story with no ending!" René emphasizes 'story' by making quotation marks in the air with her fingers.

"I just wanted to see what would come of it. Maybe nothing, maybe everything. With the attention span of the general public what it is today, maybe they won't even notice."

René stands up from the small kitchen table, grabs her empty mug and turns to face the coffee maker. "So, you want to write stories for idiots?"

"No, it's just a thought." Chuck says this more to his coffee mug than to René. He watches her as she empties the pot into her mug. "Are you going to make another pot?" He stares at the coffeemaker, as she turns around to face him.

"Do you want me to make another pot?"

Chuck looks to her face. "Yea, I've always got room for coffee. Are you gonna join me?

"I probably shouldn't but I'll just have one more cup." She walks to the table and sets her mug down next to her plate. "Don't you have any more muffins?" Chuck shakes his head no and she opens the refrigerator. Leaning forward and looking from shelf to shelf she finds two large tubs of cookie dough and some leftover Domino's pizza but no coffee. "Where's the coffee? Or don't you keep it in the fridge anymore?"

"It's in the freezer."

"The freezer? Why? Oh, never mind I don't wanna know." Closing the refrigerator door and opening the freezer she peers through the cloud of cold air billowing out at her. Squinting in the cold breeze she pushes past some tubs of Ben & Jerry's Chubby Hubby and four Tombstone frozen pizzas and grabs the large plastic bag of beans. "Didn't you tell me that plastic is bad for coffee?"

"Only if you store it at room temperature. It has to do with the PVC content of the bag and the acidity of coffee at temperatures above sixty-five degrees."

"I was kidding." René smiles. She opens the Ziploc bag and sniffs at the cold beans, sets the bag on the counter next to the refrigerator, and walks to the cupboard.

"You should get the grinder out before the coffee. Each time they warm up, they lose some of their volatile oils."

"It's only coffee! If it gets messed up, you can buy more! What the hell is with you anyway, it's like you're some kinda junkie. You don't care that you can't finish a story but your coffee better be kept safe. I'm beginning to think you're not serious about anything that matters." She opens the cupboard above the sink and gets the coffee grinder out. She lifts off the clear plastic lid and a few old grounds fall to the counter.

Chuck turns around in his seat and watches René. "I am serious about things that matter. I just happen to like fresh coffee."

"So, does it upset you when I leave the coffee out?" She points at the Ziploc bag open on the counter between the coffee maker and the grinder, turns and looks at Chuck. He meshes his fingers together in his short black hair. Moving much slower than necessary, she fills the coffee grinder with the beans.

"As a matter-of-fact it does." He gets up in an attempt to rescue his coffee from what he perceives as certain peril. René stands with her back to Chuck, between him and his beans.

René turns around, facing him. "Oh, you get up if your beans are in trouble. Why don't you take a stand for anything else?" She crosses her arms over her breasts and glares at Chuck.

"What are you talking about? Can I put those back, before they go bad?" Chuck tries to get around René by stepping to the right and changing to the left.

René catches Chuck with her arm as he steps past her. She circles around and hugs him from the back. Chuck advances toward the coffee. René holds onto him in a forceful hug that pins his upper arms to his sides. She leans her head onto his shoulder, closes her eyes, and moves her lips toward his neck. Chuck is looking at the coffee on the counter and bends forward, lifting René off her feet. "Hey! What are ya. . ." René holds fast as he carries her closer to the counter. "Damn it! If you can't think of anything—" She lets go. "—else."

Chuck stumbles forward, catching himself on the counter. "What the hell is with you anyway?"

"Me? I'm trying to kiss you and you're the one going cuckoo for coffee. What's with you?" She walks over to him and hugs him from behind again. "Are you okay? That looked really funny." She rests her head on his shoulder and kisses his neck.

René's smile fades when Chuck breaks free and steps forward to claim his prized bag of coffee. He opens the freezer and lobs the bag to safety. The bag is still open and coffee beans pour out as it arcs into the cold. Beans bounce inside the freezer and skitter onto the floor amid a chorus of clicks.

"Shit! That's just great. That was my last pound of coffee." Chuck kneels down and gathers up some of the beans. The freezer door closes with a slap above him.

René picks up her mug and coffee and pours it in the sink. She leaves the mug in the sink and steps around Chuck to the doorway and stops.

"Aren't you gonna help me?" Chuck asks.

"Help you? I wouldn't know where to begin. You don't seem to be in touch with reality, do you?"

"My reality right now is that I need to pick up these coffee beans. You could help by getting something to scoop them up with."

She looks down at Chuck. "That's not what I mean, and you know it." She looks from Chuck's face to a lone bean on the floor. She reaches out her foot and crunches the bean under her shoe.

Chuck looks up at her, aghast. "If you don't wanna help, I understand I guess — but you don't have to make more of mess, you know?"

"More of a mess? I think you're missing my point."

"Your point? I don't even know what the hell you're talking about. So I guess I did 'miss' it. Right now, I'm just trying to clean up some spilled coffee beans."

"When in fact you should be trying to keep me from leaving."

"Leaving?"

"Yes, I don't know why the hell you are so concerned with that damned coffee. A few minutes ago I was kissing you."

"You were and your point is…"

René sighs. "You remember. I think that's even worse than if you didn't remember."

"What do you mean?"

"I don't think you care about reality Chuck. You don't seem to notice me anymore. All you seem to care about is coffee. You don't even care about writing."

"But I couldn't write if I didn't have any coffee."

"You can't write anyway."

"What?"

"You heard me. I said you can't write anyway and you don't give a damn about me." René turns and walks out of the kitchen.

Chuck stands up, looks at the remnants of the bean René stepped on, and tries to figure out what she meant. He hears the front door open and whispers, "Wait."

As he hears the door close he throws the beans he had collected into the garbage can and walks out of the kitchen.

AUTHOR BIOS

JACK BERGQUIST is a native Bostonian, who fell in love with California at age six and made the migration seven years ago. He now resides in Alameda, CA with his wife and daughter, and teaches at an Oakland middle school. His writing crossing from fiction and non-fiction to screenwriting.

LIVIA CHING-GERRING primarily writes lyrical creative nonfiction essays. Livia's personal and professional writing has appeared in The Fempire (www. thefempire.com), Clean Sheets Magazine, the Open Process Series at Intersection for the Arts in San Francisco, Audrey Magazine, Beeswax Magazine, GamePro Magazine, Hyphen Magazine, Shonen Jump Magazine and others. She has won scholarships through the California College of the Arts and the 2008 Highlights Foundation Writers Workshop at Chautauqua, New York. Livia is also the owner and founder of Unicorn Turds Gallery, part of the 25th Street Collective located in Oakland, California.(www.unicornturds.com)

SHELANA DESILVA is a grantwriter for a national environmental organization that builds parks in cities and conserves open space throughout the United States. She also freelances as a curmudgeonly editor, though she is very easy to work with provided you don't quibble about commas. Her work has appeared on AlterNet.org, in *Beeswax Magazine*, and in *Lip Magazine*. She received a MFA in Writing from California College of the Arts in 2007 and has a background in sticking it to the man. Someday, she hopes to leave the glamour of Oakland, California behind for a life of spear-fishing and trading coconuts for wine.

LYNDSEY ELLIS is a writer and aspiring author. She was a participant in the 7th Annual Intergenerational Writers' Lab at the Intersection for the Arts in San Francisco, CA and Vermont Studio Center residency program. She's a fellowship recipient of the Summer Literary Seminars Program in Nairobi, Kenya, and she has led creative writing workshops at the African American Art & Culture Complex in San Francisco, CA. Her writing appears in *Know the Names of Things Literary Anthology, Synchronized Chaos, Indigest, Write This, Community Voices,* Examiner.com, AND Magazine, Western Edition Community Newspapers, and Napa Valley News Online. A native of St. Louis MO, Ellis currently lives in Oakland, CA.

ANDREW GORI grew up surrounded by books in a small town north east of New York City. As a freelance journalist he has covered travel, the arts, technology, health and education, and his collected works of fiction can be found scattered around his San Francisco apartment.

JASON KOLBRICH is in a long-term relationship with the written word, writing his first short story when he was nine years old. There have been a few spats over the years but many good times too. They have recently built a house together and we are all eagerly awaiting the announcement of some children. He earned an MFA in Creative Writing at California College of Arts and Crafts where he also learned that a capitalistic system does not shower poets with money. He has traveled over much of the US and lived abroad. He currently lives, works and writes in the San Francisco Bay Area.

ANNE LYNCH lives in Atlanta where she works at Georgia Tech and runs a Hungarian club that she founded in 2004. She has been recognized by the Hungarian Ambassador for her work bringing together the Hungarian Community in Georgia. Anne has her BA with High Honors in Creative Writing from Emory University and her MFA in Creative Writing from the California College of the Arts. She has proofread an academic book "The Limes of Pannonia" about Roman ruins in Hungary as well as a collection of work by award-winning transgender performance artist Scott Turner Schofield. Ms. Lynch is working on her first screenplay.

MYRON MICHAEL is a recording artist, writing teacher, and Cave Canem Fellowship recipient. His words appear online and in Days I Moved Through Ordinary Sounds (City Lights), Nanomajority, Fourteen Hills, Harvard Review online, and Toad Suck Review, respectively. His chapbook *Scatter Plot* won the 2010 Willow Books Integral Music Chapbook Prize, and he is co-author of *Hang Man* (Move Or Die, 2010). He lives in the Bay Area where he curates HELIOTROPE, a monthly reading series.

ADAM MOSKOWITZ lived in Spain for a short time during his early twenties. He was afraid his English was going, and started reading more books than ever before. He started writing essays soon after, got his MFA, and is currently working on fiction. Adam has been a middle and high school teacher in the Bay Area since 2005.

NANA K. TWUMASI was born in Texas, and raised in a bunch of other places, which left her with a midwest work-ethic, an east-coast attitude and, now that she lives in Oakland, CA, a west-coast sense of time. Her work has appeared in *Sou'wester*, as part of Ballyhoo Stories' 50 States Project, and the International Museum of Women's *Imagining Ourselves* online exhibit. In her spare time, she co-edits *Monday Night*, a journal of new literature (www.mondaynightlit.com)